INTERNET MARKETING TO GO

I0503187

Ca$hing in on Article Writing

By Jinger Jarrett

Disclaimer – Every care has gone into making sure the information provided in this book is true and correct. Any incorrect information is solely the responsibility of the author.

Create Space/Amazon ISBN: 1438229194

EAN-139781438229195

Contents

Introduction

Although I have tried many methods for marketing my business on the internet, I haven't found a more successful marketing technique than writing articles. No other marketing method can combine several marketing techniques into one the way writing articles can.

Before I tell you why, let me explain something.

Everyone is different, and although the way I teach article writing will work for anyone who is willing to learn, not every marketing technique is the right technique for every marketer.

The reason why is your own personal belief. You must first believe that the marketing technique you are using will work for you. Once you have chosen how you will market, then you need to learn everything you can about the marketing technique you are using. Become an expert using that marketing technique, whatever it is, and you will be very successful at it.

Now, with that in mind, here is what article writing and promotion will do for you:

1. It will brand you as an expert in your field.

Why is this so important?

In his book, ***"How to Become a Recognized Expert in Your Field in 60 Days or Less"***, author Robert Bly says that when you brand yourself as an expert, customers will come to you. This will cut your marketing costs to nothing, and not only that, you can concentrate on creating new products, as well as other activities that will help you dramatically increase your income.

This is the real secret to website conversion: driving targeted traffic to your website. Potential customers who come to you are targeted traffic, traffic that is looking for what you are selling. When you brand yourself as an expert, you will drive targeted traffic to your website because visitors are looking for what you are offering.

2. You build valuable backlinks.

You can quickly and easily build thousands of backlinks pointing back to your website, and you can do this in a very short time.   Write a good article about something that others want to know about, and other webmasters will publish your article on their websites. With thousands of backlinks pointing back to your website, not only will others more easily find you, but you will raise your rankings in the search engines.

3. You make your business viral.

Years after you've written an article, it will continue to drive traffic to your site without you having to do anything. The less work you have to do to market your site, the better off you will be because you'll be able to focus your attention on other money making activities within your business.

Although I've only written over 100+ articles over the last few years that I've been using articles to market my business, this is what article writing and promotion has accomplished for me:

I have thousands of backlinks pointing back to my websites.

My articles have been featured in just about all of the top ezines on the internet, ezines that have readerships that rival the top newspapers in the United States.

I've received emails from readers in over 40 countries throughout the world.

My articles have been featured in several print publications, including books, newspapers, and magazines worldwide.

I've made thousands of dollars I wouldn't have made if I hadn't written the articles.

The bottom line is that if you want an effective marketing method to market your business that combines all of the best free internet marketing strategies into one, then look no further. Article writing and promotion is what you are looking for.

Before you start the course, you need to download your tools and ebooks. You can find them here: **http://www.jingerjarrett.com/downloadpages/articlew ritingecourse.html**. You will also want to join my list so that you can get course updates. You'll receive each of the lessons in your email, as well as future updates.

Now, let's get started.

Lesson 1
Getting Ideas

Article ideas are everywhere. You can read articles, product reviews, and other websites that relate to your products and services to help you find ideas for your articles.

If you can't find an article idea for your product, then you have the wrong product.

Let me stress here that one of the most important things you need to do when starting your business is to choose something you feel passionate about.

I know that conventional wisdom says that you should choose a profitable niche. However, I also believe that you should choose a profitable niche on something you feel passionate about and like to talk about.

So, your first step is to go to several article directories and find articles on your topic.

Here are two that have lots of articles:

http://www.ezinearticles.com

Read several articles on your topic. Write down any ideas that you get.

This can be anything from how you could write the article better to an idea for an article of your own.

Once you have made your notes, your next step will be to do a topic search in the search engines and gather information.

This is especially important for those new to writing articles because you need to make sure that you fully understand your subject.

As an internet marketer and writer, I get ideas for my articles just from reading my email.

I once wrote an article that was published in Site Pro News simply because I noticed that one of the articles published by one of their writers had out of date information.

I sent my article to the publisher, and he published my article.

It's important that you keep a notebook, text file, or whatever you need to keep track of your notes on article writing.

I use a text file to jot down ideas while I'm working. I also add links, and any other notes I need to add. This speeds up the article writing process. Sometimes a complete outline for an article will fall out of my head, and I write that down too.

The point is, there are thousands of article ideas out there, and one of them has your name on it.

If you need organizers, or any type of writing software, as well as tools to help you track your articles, you'll find the best ones here: **http://www.freewarehome.com**. Look under tools for

writers.

You should also study your product or service. Read the sales copy. This is especially important if you are selling affiliate programs or MLM. Make sure that you understand all of the benefits and features of your product.

If you haven't bought a copy, now is the time. Reading the product will also help you come up with even more ideas, not only for writing articles about it, but for promoting it.

Another way to find article ideas is to search for article directories on your topic. Make sure you bookmark these so that you can go back to them later.

Finally, one tool that I think you will find to be indispensible is the **Public Domain Toolbar**. This will give you thousands of resources on Public Domain Information. In the final bonus lesson, we'll talk about using Public Domain information to help you write articles.

http://www.publicdomainforum.com

(You'll need to subscribe to this site to get the materials, but it's free. I've been a member for years, and the resources are excellent.)

That's it for today. By now, you should have several ideas for your article.

Let me stress that whenever you get an idea, whether it's for a new article, or anything else, WRITE IT DOWN.

Assignment #1

1. Do a search for articles on your topic. Read the articles. Make notes about these articles. What can you do better? What kinds of ideas do these articles spark for you?

2. Do a topical search. I recommend Google because Google is the most comprehensive search engine on the internet. Read product reviews, articles, forums, and any other information you find on

your topic. Make notes.

3. If you need more information, search for article directories on your topic.

4. Read product reviews and the sales letter for your product. Write down the features and benefits of your product. If you don't own the product, buy it.

5. Download the Public Domain Toolbar. You can use public domain information to help you write articles, as well as find ideas for articles.

Notes

Lesson 2
Choosing a Title

Before you start this lesson, I recommend you go back to the introduction and download the tools I have created for you. (This page is regularly updated to bring you the latest, so check there when you need tools to help you with your article writing. You will find an article creator, as well as other tools and resources to help you.)

Now, the first thing you need to do to start this lesson is to download a copy of the software **Headline Creator Pro**. This tool will save you hours and hours of time in crafting good titles for your article. You don't have to use the titles you create. What this software will do is help you get ideas.

I know you will use this tool over and over not just for your articles, but for anything else you write that you need a title for.

There are several things you want to consider when choosing a title for your article.

Length - You want your title to be as short and catchy as possible. Make it descriptive. You want it to fully describe what your article is about in as few words as possible. However, there will be times when a longer title is more suitable. It's up to you to judge when this is necessary.

Type of Headline Format - A title is no different from a headline. Some examples of headline formats are:

How To - You are telling the person how to do something. This generally includes some kind of steps. For example:

How to Make Money on the Internet

Lists - This is both an article format, as well as a title format. You are listing a group of things that are similar, or related. For example:

58 Ways to Make Money Now

The Question - Ask your reader a question. The key here is to make sure that you get an answer that makes the reader want to read further. For example:

Do you want to make more money today?

Curiosity - You are seeking to grab the reader's attention. Be careful here though; your title must be descriptive enough of your article to make your reader want to read it. For example:

Always A Bridesmaid, Never A Bride

News - In this type of title, your title is similar to what you would see in a news story or a press release. If you choose this type of title, be sure and study very carefully several newspapers, as well as press releases. For example:

Announcing... The New Edition Of The Encyclopedia That Makes It Fun To Learn Things

You want to make your title intriguing, provocative and attention getting. You want the reader to read on.

You can use Headline Creator Pro to help you craft headlines and titles. Keep a swipe file of these. Put them in a text document, or if you are really organized, use a spreadsheet or database program.

I also recommend that if you are writing an article for a magazine, instead of for promotion, that you study your favorite magazines. Choose the titles you like and modify them for your own use. Study what works.

Use your swipe file to help you generate ideas for titles. Modify, don't copy, ideas you have in your swipe files.

For example, you can take the title, "58 Ways to Make Money Now", and change it to "5 Ways to Write Better Articles".

And that's the title of the article I'll be writing for you in this ecourse.

Finally, one thing I consider absolutely crucial in writing your titles, especially if you are planning to use your articles as a promotional tool online, is to make sure you include your keywords in your title. You will want to do your keyword research BEFORE you write your titles.

The purpose of doing keyword research is to help your articles rank higher in the search engines. This will get you more traffic.

Now, I won't take the time here to explain how to do keyword research. I've fully explained that in my book, "Internet Marketing for Free: The GUIDE." You can download a copy from the tools page and read the chapter on search engine optimization, and you'll know everything you need to know about keyword research.

Assignment #2

1. Research to find ideas for titles. You want to find at least five ideas for article titles. Make sure that if you find any ideas you want to go back to later, that you start a swipe file and add these ideas to it. You can find possible title ideas in article directories like Ezine Articles. You can also use Headline Creator Pro.

2. Write five titles for possible articles. The important point to remember is that you can change your title later. Sometimes I do. Include your keywords in your title.

Please feel free to use my articles to help you get ideas, as well as help you write titles for your articles. You'll find my articles available for download at my affiliate site: http://affiliates.smallbusinesshowto.com, or you can read them at my blog: http://www.askjinger.com.

Here is one more resource I want you to be aware of: the High Rankings Forum. Not only can you get some great writing tips, but you can learn about optimizing your articles for the search engines so that they rank higher.

http://www.highrankings.com/forum/

Notes

Lesson 3
Formula for Success

Now it's time to get to the good stuff: writing your article.

For those of you who have written articles before, this formula may seem simplistic. However, it is a quick and easy way to help you write a good article. For those who haven't written articles before, this will show you how easy it really is to write one.

First, I want to talk about length because as writers, we love to write, and we're in love with what we have to say.

Once you master the technique of article writing though, you can turn out a quality article in a very short time. Some of my articles have been written in 15 minutes or less and have flowed out onto the page after simmering in my head for awhile.

Now, if you are using articles to promote yourself on the Internet, your article should be in the range of 500 - 700 words, although many sites will accept articles that are as little as 400 words. 500 – 700 words is the average length that most publishers are looking for in their newsletters. For web sites, it just depends on the webmaster.

I personally don't care how long the article is. If I like the writer and the writing, I'll publish it regardless of the length.

If you are writing an article for pay for either an offline or online magazine or ezine, you'll need to consider the publication. Each publication has its own guidelines for how long your article should be.

I know I've said this before, but I will say it again: study your market, the publication you want to publish in, etc. One of the biggest complaints publishers have is all the material they get that is unsuitable for their publications.

Let's face it. Publishers are busy. They don't have time to wade through mountains of stuff that's a waste of their time. If you want them to remember you kindly and want them to publish you again and again, then give them an article they want.

Now, there are two types of articles I'm focusing on because these article types are the easiest to write.

Those types of articles are: lists and recipes.

A list is an article where you offer several related items and then explain each one. A recipe is where you give step by step directions on how to do something. In other words, a how to.

Going back to lesson 2 we chose a title for our article. In my case, the article I will be showing you how to write is "5 Ways to Write Better Articles".

(In this lesson, instead of having an exercise at the end, we'll be working your exercise throughout this lesson).

So, at the top of your text document, notepad, or whatever, start with the title.

Here is mine again: 5 Ways to Write Better Articles.

Next, underneath it, you will write down your ideas. In my case, I need 5 ideas here to complete my article.

For example:

1. Stick to your subject.

2. Read it out loud.

3. Do a spell check and check your links.

4. Write about things other people want to know about.

5. Give your readers good information.

Now, I wrote these off the top of my head. There's a reason for this. Right now, I am showing you development. The beauty of writing in a text document is that you can cut and paste and move things around, which we will be doing.

With my five ideas, I now move them around to look like this:

4. Write about things other people want to know about.

5. Give your readers good information.

1. Stick to your subject.

3. Do a spell check and check your links.

2. Read it out loud.

By moving my 5 ideas around, I have an article that is more chronological and makes more sense. At this point, you can go back and renumber everything to the correct order, so now we have:

5 Ways to Write Better Articles

1. Write about things other people want to know about.

2. Give your readers good information.

3. Stick to your subject.

4. Do a spell check and check your links.

5. Read it out loud.

You now have the basic frame for your article. In the next lesson, we'll finish writing your article using this simple article writing formula.

If you like, you can outline several different articles this way so that you have several articles in the works. This variety will help you in your writing and give you a constant flow of ideas.

Assignment #3

1. As illustrated in the lesson above, you now outline the basic, major points of an article. A tool you may find to be very handy is Note Tab Lite. This is a tabbed text editor. It's what I use when I write my articles.

You'll find it here, and it's free: **http://www.notetab.com/**.

You can also download the free article writing software from my website. This software will take you step by step through the article writing process.

Lesson 4
Resources Boxes, Formatting and Promoting Your Article

After the title, the most important element of your article is the resource box. This is where you will promote your business and get readers to visit your site.

Like classified advertising, this is a two step process: you want to give readers an incentive for visiting your site.

Your incentive can be a free ebook, ecourse, ezine, free software, or whatever you want. Be creative. Offer something no one else is offering, something that will get the reader to click through.

What's important is that your site offers more information on the topic you've written about in your article. Your article is only a taste. The meal should be on your site.

For example, here is a resource box that I have created for one of my sites:

****

Jinger Jarrett will show you "How to REALLY Start Your Business in 30 Days". Free ecourse includes step by step instructions and all the tools you need to build your business, and its free.
http://www.smallbusiness.com

****

Try to keep your resource box to 250 characters. HTML resource boxes should be no more than 500 characters. You're promoting your business, not giving your life story.

This may sound confusing, but it's really not. Once you format your resource box, you'll know if it's too long or not.

You may even want to write one even shorter than this one because some publishers only allow your resource box to be three lines long.

Once you've written your resource box, it's time to check your article and resource box. You will determine your word count, which some publishers will want in order to determine if they will publish your article or not.

This is the tool I use to check the length of my articles and resource boxes, and it's free: **http://www.fwointl.com/ FWOFormatter.html**

Format your resource box separately from your article so that you get an accurate word count.

Next, create a text document for your article. If you're using the article writing software, it will do all of this for you. Then all you have to do is save it. If you're using a text editor, you will want to put the parts of your document in the following order as this is the way most article directories are formatted: title, summary, article, resource box (include both the text and HTML versions), and keywords.

For example, if you are using "My Article Submitter" software, or you are submitting through Article Marketer, this is the order you will copy the elements into the software or into the Article Marketer submission form.

You'll also use this document to copy and paste from so that it's faster to submit your article. (You can also use Roboform to help you post your articles. You can get a copy of Roboform Magic for free to show you how to submit articles, ads, and other marketing materials faster. Join my members' site for free and download this from the bonuses page: **http:// www.killermarketingarsenal.com/ezine/**).

Once you've finished writing your article, your resource box, and it's properly formatted, it's time to start promoting your article.

There are several ways that you can do this:

1. **Article Marketer** - http://www.jingerjarrett.com/recommends/article-marketer.html - This site offers one click submission of your article. You can use the free version, and it will send your article to about 30 different article directories and 12,000 different publishers. You can also upgrade to the paid version. This will put your article in thousands of directories, as well as in front of thousands of publishers. You won't find a faster, easier way to submit your articles. You can even automate your submissions to go out when you want them to, basically putting your article submissions on autopilot.

2. **Article Dashboard Forum** - http://www.articledashboard.com/forum/ - You'll find tons of article directories on this site. All you have to do is browse the forum.

3. **Internet Marketing Directories** - http://www.arcanaweb.com/resources/article-directories.html -

You'll find hundreds of article directories on this site, including lots of niches directories where you can submit articles on specific topics, like dogs.

4. **Directory of Article Directories** - http://www.directoryofarticledirectories.com/ - Offers a nice collection of article directories. Look here to find more niche directories you can add to the My Article Submitter software.

5. **Top Ranking Article Directories**

http://www.ezinearticles.com

http://www.goarticles.com

http://www.ideamarketers.com

http://www.marketing-seek.com

http://www.articlecity.com

http://www.articlecodex.com – Use this website to syndicate your articles on hundreds of article directories throughout the internet, or use it to create your own automated article directory on your website.

http://www.articleoverdrive.com – This is another site where you can syndicate your articles across a lot of sites. You can also use it to create your own instantly updated article directories on your sites so you can add thousands of content pages to your sites.

Let me give you a tip here: if you use Article Marketer to market your articles through the paid account, you get such wide distribution, including Ezine Articles and Go Articles, that it's not really necessary to do a lot of submission somewhere else. The only other sites I submit to after I submit my article at Article Marketer are:

Article Dashboard – http://www.articledashboard.com

Search Warp – http://www.searchwarp.com

Self Growth – http://www.selfgrowth.com

Self Growth is a great site to submit to because it allows you to brand yourself as an expert. If your article is really good, then you could be featured in the newsletter, which goes out to over 950,000 subscribers.

6. **Submission Software**

My Article Submitter -
http://www.jingerjarrett.com/recommends/myfreegiveaway.html - You can get this software absolutely free through My Free Giveaway. You can use it to keep track of all of the Article Directory sites you submit to, as well as to submit your articles. It will cut hours and hours off of your submissions, and you can submit to only the sites you want to.

Article Distributor - http://www.after5webdesign.com/software.html - You can use this software to submit your articles to Article Dashboard sites. It really speeds up your article submission process. You can also use this software to submit your profile on these sites. This allows you to promote multiple sites, increasing your backlinks, as well as your presence on the internet. This software is constantly updated, and it's completely free.

Assignment #4

1. Write your resource box. If you are having trouble, refer back to mine, or search the article directories and study the article directories to help you write one.

2. Format your article. You want to check your word count to make sure your article is long enough. Also, write both a text version and an HTML formatted version of your resource box. Your article format within your text document should be as follows: Title, Summary, Article, Text Resource Box, HTML Resource Box, Keywords. If you use the article writing software, it will automatically do this formatting for you.

3. Once you have a text document with all of your information, choose your directories. Start with those that rank highest on Alexa. Submit to as many directories as you can.

Lesson 5
Public Domain Information, Private Label Articles, and Duplicate Content

Although I use the articles of others on my websites, I seldom use public domain or private label articles. The reason why is that it's very hard to find public domain information on small business and internet marketing.

With private label articles, although I believe they are excellent for helping to build content rich, original websites, I don't think they have any place in promotional article writing unless you plan to fully rewrite them.

Most people who use private label articles to promote themselves don't do it right. Not only do they waste their own time, they waste the time of publishers.

Most publishers won't accept private label articles out of the box because they've seen them before. Publishing the exact same article under different names leads to copyright issues because "article writers" who submit private label articles don't bother to customize the articles. Submitting these articles without thorough rewrites leads others to question your credibility, as well as questioning whether or not you really are an expert on your topic.

If you are trying to brand yourself as an expert, this strategy will backfire. Instead, you'll be branded as an amateur. Once you destroy your reputation on the internet, it's very hard to get back.

Now, let me explain what public domain, private label, and duplicate content are and how you can use them effectively.

First, public domain information is any information that has expired copyright or no copyright at all. It can also include all kinds of publications created by the government as much of this information is public domain This information can be freely used.

However, before using any content that is considered public domain, you should check to make sure there is no copyright on the work you want to use. If you are using government information, check for the guidelines for use. Guidelines should be provided on the site where you find the material.

Do a rewrite of the information. Truly make it your own. Make it original by adding to it, changing it, and improving on the material you are using. Then the work becomes what is called a derivative work, and you can copyright it.

Public domain is better for helping you build a content rich website. Unless you completely rewrite the material for an article, you run the risk of someone coming back and accusing you of plagiarism or maybe even copyright violation. It's not worth destroying your credibility online.

The same applies to private label articles. When using articles to promote yourself, too many people are using them to build links back to their sites. If you aren't using articles to build credibility and expertise in your topic, you're really wasting your time.

When people see the same article over and over under a different name, then they see it for what it is: a writer who is too lazy to write his/her own articles. You will fail to do what article writing really should do: prove you are an expert and know what you are talking about.

Another mistake here is sending out private label articles on different topics totally unrelated to your site. When readers get to the end of an article, they expect to refer them to a website with more information and resources. If your site isn't related to the content of the article, readers will click away and go somewhere else in search of more information.

With private label articles, you need to rewrite at least 25 to 50 percent of the content before you can even use it as your own material. I've found it faster to just write my own articles, and then they are completely unique. My own articles brand me, show my expertise, and help drive traffic to my site because my articles are related to my offerings.

(Since I wrote the original version of this ebook, I have found a way to use private label articles when I don't have any ideas for articles. I use a tool called Dupe Free Pro, **http://www.dupefreepro.com**. This tool allows me to rewrite the original PLR article into my own words and then do a comparison of the original article to my version. It makes article writing really fast, and you can rewrite an article in just a few minutes. You can download the software for free just by signing up for the list on this site.)

Finally, let's discuss duplicate content.

There are actually two kinds of duplicate content. One is OK, and the other is not.

It is somewhat hard to define what duplicate content really is because everyone seems to have his/her own definitions about what duplicate content really is.

I would define black hat duplicate content as mirror sites, that is, sites that have the same exact same content under different domains.

This would also be things like out of the box websites that haven't been customized, or out of the box sites, like Adsense websites people buy and don't change. Often, the only difference in these sites is the domain name.

This is a mistake because the search engines pick them up easily and delete them.

I'm not saying you shouldn't use duplicate content. Duplicate content is useful on your website if the content you are using is valuable for your readers.

Unfortunately, because of so many broad definitions of duplicate content, many webmasters have been frightened into buying all kinds of unnecessary tools to avoid what is called the "duplicate content penalty".

The truth is, if duplicate content were completely banned, Google, Yahoo, and MSN would all have to ban themselves. After all, they are all made up of news, articles, and content from other resources, and none of it is original.

However, what Google, Yahoo, and MSN are trying to do is to present all relevant offerings on a topic. That's what search engines are for. Therefore, they include all related resources.

This is how your website should be structured. If your topic is fitness equipment, you want to offer articles, reviews, resources, and links to fitness equipment. You want your coverage of the topic to be as exhaustive as possible. You can make your site an authority site by having as much content as possible and customizing your site as much as possible.

This is good duplicate content because it offers value to your visitors, and this is what the search engines are looking for. In other words, your content doesn't have to be completely original; it is more important to offer value to your visitors.

Ultimately, to get a page to rank high in the site engines, it does have to be original. However, many of my articles rank higher on other sites than they do on mine because they've been picked up by sites I have no chance of ever competing against no matter how much I optimize my site.

This is fine. I'll still be found for those keywords because my article will be at the top of the search engines for those keywords.

The bad form of duplicate content can be where you create a website, buy several different domains, and then redirect all of those domains to the one site. Another form of this is creating mirror sites where you upload the same site under different domains.

Another example of duplicate content that is bad is redirects. If the topic of your website is health, but you are redirecting your website visitors to a gambling site, or some other site that is totally unrelated, then you are cheating your visitors. The search engines will penalize you.

It's not wrong to use redirects. I use them all of the time. In fact, the search engines don't have a problem with legitimate redirects where you are trying to protect your affiliate links, or where pages on your site have changed and you are sending visitors to the correct page.

However, when you use redirects, use them for the right purpose. Don't cheat your visitors for the sake of a commission or because you're in this only to make money. Your visitors will see straight through it and go elsewhere.

Again, it's about purpose.

The last example I want to mention are what I call "junk sites". These are sites that are created with certain types of scripts or software. These scripts and software generate thousands of keyword pages with no real content on them except Google Adsense, Yahoo headlines, and maybe an ad.

This violates the Google terms of service, as well as Yahoo's terms of service because Yahoo does not allow its news headlines to be displayed on commercial sites.

What you should understand here is that the you should never use any kind of techniques that are only about commercial gain and provide no real value to your potential customers. Your customers are your lifeblood in your business.

Show them respect. They deserve it. You should never trick your visitor for the sake of a sale.

Tricks will only destroy your reputation. You might make a lot of money for a short time, but if you own a real business, you're in it for the long term. Once your reputation online is gone, it's gone. You won't ever get it back.

The techniques I've just discussed are what is called "Black Hat" in search engine optimization. The techniques you want to use are called "White Hat". Use "White Hat" techniques, and you'll build credibility and trust among your visitors, as well as high search engine rankings.

That's the topic of our next lesson.

Assignment #5

If you've decided you would like to try using PLR or public domain materials to help you supplement your regular writing, then it's time to do a search for these materials.

The easiest way to do this is to download the Public Domain toolbar. You can get it here: **http://www.publicdomainforum.com/**. You will need to sign up for Charles's list, but it's free. You'll receive instructions on downloading the toolbar, as well as access to the forum where you can sign up for an account.

You can also do a search in the search engines for public domain. Search for public domain, free public domain, or some other keyword combination.

With PLR, I am really loathe to recommend any particular site because it depends on your topic. Your best bet is to search the search engines for topics like these: free PLR, free private label rights, free private label rights articles, etc. You'll find plenty of sites that offer private label rights. You can also check my blog to for free private label rights as I sometimes find stuff I like. You'll find it here: **http://www.askjinger.com.**

Lesson 6
Articles and Search Engine Optimization

Although I'm about to teach you how to optimize your articles for the search engines, the optimization techniques that I discuss can be used for any page on your website.

The one mistake I made when I first started marketing on the internet was not learning search engine optimization. The big name "gurus" never talked about it. All of their marketing strategies revolved around spending money, and all they did was transfer corresponding offline techniques to the online world.

That's fine if you have a lot of money to market online, but what if you don't?

I spent thousands of dollars reading all of the gurus' stuff, but in the end, I learned that I could market my business on the internet for free, and that there were certain techniques, like article writing and search engine optimization, which are all free, that I could use instead of trying to follow their marketing methods, which are nothing but rehased offline techniques anyway. What I want to stress here is to learn one or two internet marketing techniques and master them. Apply them to your business consistently, and you will succceed.

What this really means for your bottom line, your income, is that you will have to do a little learning. The result is that it will pay off for you by increasing your business profits and ridding you of the unnecessary business expenses of marketing.

To optimize your articles for the search engines means that you will need three tools to get you started. All of these tools are free.

1. **Web CEO** - http://www.smallbusinesshowto.com/search.html - This search engine optimization suite is free. It works on both Windows and MAC. It includes all of the documentation you need to learn search engine optimization, as well as telling you what you need to do to optimize your page. If you are anxious to get started, then I recommend you read the quickstart guide.

You'll have your search engine optimization campaign up and running within one hour.

2. **Keyword Buzz** - http://www.imbuzzcreators.com/ - This software will help you find the right keywords to target in your articles. You can also use Web CEO to help you find keywords. I like Keyword Buzz because it's so easy to use. The advantage of using Web CEO is that you'll get a clear picture of all of the searches done on a keyword globally. What this means is Web CEO uses keyword information from across the globe with a wide variety of search engines.

3. **Text2HTML** - http://www.cyber-matrix.com/txt2html.html - This software will convert your text to HTML so that you can optimize it.

You will need to set up these software programs on your computer. Once you've set up the software, then it's time to start working on your article.

BEFORE you write your article, you will need to do a search for your keywords. Once you have done a search for the keywords on your topic, then select the keywords you want to use. Write down the number of times that your keywords have been searched for.

Go to MSN, put your keyword phrase in quotes, and then search for it. Write down the number of pages that are in MSN for your keyword search term. This will be at the top of the results page.

You're probably wondering why I chose MSN.

According to Rob Benwell of "Blogging to the Bank", MSN updates faster than Yahoo or Google, giving you more accurate results on how many sites there are that have optimized for a particular keyword. The difference between an optimized keyword phrase, and a keyword phrase that hasn't been optimized is when you use the quotes. The search engines will search for that particular phrase.

The formula for determining how competitive your keyword phrase is, as follows:

RESULTS / SEARCHES X 10 = KEYWORD EFFECTIVENESS INDEX

For example, a search of internet marketing reveals the following:

RESULTS = 9,876,097

SEARCHES = 290,015

X 10 = 34.537.......

The closer the number is to 1, the less competition you will have, and the easier it will be to optimize your page for the keyword, as well as get to the first three pages of search results.

Once you've found a keyword, or keyword phrase, then it's time to write your article. I've already explained in detail how to write your article in the previous lessons.

What's important here is that you make sure you include your keyword phrase in the title of your article, as well as several times throughout the body of your article. Don't go crazy though. If you include it too many times, your article will be seen as keyword spamming.

Once you've written your article, then you can use the TXT2HTML tool to convert your article to HTML. When you've converted your article to HTML, then you can use Web CEO to help you further optimize your article.

Now you have a search engine optimized article that you can add to your website, as well as send out to article directories and other webmasters. All you have to do is open the article in your browser. If you are using IE, click on "View", and then click on "Source". Copy the text between the <body> and </body tags. Then take this code and paste it into your website page.

You'll send out your article in text, which means your article won't be as optimized as it could be. However, you'll have your article search engine optimized for your site, which will help you raise your rankings in the search engines. If you post to Search Warp, or other sites that allow you to use HTML in your articles, you can use search engine optimization techniques to improve the ranking of your article. Remember though, don't include links in your article unless you're using it on your site. Most article directories don't allow links of any kind in the body of the article.

There's one other area I'd like to address here, and that's syndication.

Many of the newer autoresponders, including the ones at **Ultimate Marketing Center**, http://www.jingerjarrett.com/recommends/ultimatem arketingcenter.html, have an RSS feed. What this allows you to do is syndicate your articles through RSS readers.

It also allows you to syndicate your articles to websites.

What you need to do is set up an autoresponder that has an RSS feed. Allow readers to subscribe to your list. Every time you write an article, send it out through the list and archive the article so that it shows up in the RSS feed. This way, sites that syndicate your RSS feed will have constantly updating content from your website, and you will not only gain more backlinks, but you will have a way to easily get your articles and content on other sites.

If an RSS autoresponder isn't available to you, your articles can still be syndicated through RSS provided you submit your articles to sites that use RSS. Ezine Articles is one example of sites that use RSS. There are others. Just check the site before you submit.

Assignment # 6

Optimizing your article for the search engine is easy. All you have to do is follow the steps for optimizing it.

1. Select your keywords or keyword phrases you want to use and then write your article.

2. Convert your article to HTML using the HTML converter.

3. Load your article into Web CEO and have Web CEO analyze it. Web CEO will tell you what you need to do to optimize your article for the search engines. Click on "Go" in the bottom left of the Web CEO window. This will bring up the control panel. Go to "Optimize Pages" under "Find Your Niche", and load your page to optimize it.

Bonus Lesson
Bum Marketing

When I originally wrote this report, Bum Marketing didn't exist, or at least it wasn't called that. Times have changed, and if you want to get the most out of your article writing and promotional efforts, Bum Marketing should be a crucial part of your education.

If you want to use Bum Marketing as a way to make more money from you articles, and it will help you make more money, then I would recommend you take my $100 a Day ecourse. It's free, and it will explain in detail how to use your articles with Bum Marketing. Below are some things I didn't include in the course I'd like to share with you here.

First, Bum Marketing is about creating and promoting articles as little sales machines for your business. You write as many articles as you possibly can on the topics you are interested in, and then submit them to the article directories. You don't have to have a website to do Bum Marketing.

However, most article directories won't accept your articles unless you have a website.

The easiest way around this is to create Squidoo lenses. Squidoo lenses are mini websites with links to resources on the topic. This can include You Tube videos, Ebay, Amazon, as well as news and blog sites, or any links you add. You can also write an article or two as well as include your own resources.

Squidoo lenses are easy to create, and you can do one in a few minutes. Although Squidoo lenses are great for promoting affiliate programs and making money from both Squidoo and the affiliate programs you promote, you can also promote your own products and services. Lenses rank very high in the search engines and can get you a lot of traffic to your business.

You need to sign up, but it's free: **http://www.jingerjarrett.com/recommends/squidoolens.html**

There are plenty of resources on this site to show you how to promote your Squidoo lenses, and you can even turn Squidoo into a business.

For more information on using Squidoo, you can take my free ecourse: **http://www.askjinger.com/squidoo/**.

Another option here is to build a blog. Blogger and Wordpress are both good options here. The advantage of Wordpress over Blogger is future posting. The advantage of

Blogger is that it's a Google property and Blogger blogs tend to rank high in the search engines.

For more information:

Wordpress – http://www.wordpress.com

Blogger – http://www.blogger.com

If you don't want the hassles of building a website, you still have options with your article writing.

You can submit your article to either of these two directories, and they allow you to put affiliate links in your resource box.

With Go Articles, you can also submit product reviews, so if you are marketing affiliate programs, you can also write product reviews and submit those too. Product reviews are popular online because those searching the search engines are looking for more information. You can give them more information with your product reviews.

Go Articles – http://www.goarticles.com

Article City – http://www.articlecity.com

I personally prefer Go Articles over Article City because Article City wants your articles to be exclusive, and they don't allow you to write product reviews. It also takes anywhere from 14 days to 30 days to get your articles accepted. Go Articles accepts your articles and product reviews immediately.

What I would recommend is that you start off by writing articles for Go Articles. Submit as many as you can. When you have time, write a few articles for Article City and get them submitted there.

Finally, maybe you have some type of premade website, or you want to promote an affiliate program without building a website. Because many sites, like Ezine Articles, won't accept affiliate links in the resource box, you need a way to get around this. Ezine Articles is the top article directory on the internet, and you really do want to put your articles here.

The way around for this is to buy a domain and point it at the program or site you are promoting. Make sure you use the domain cloaking feature so that the domain shows in the address box of the browser.

This technique is very effective, and writer Jason DeVelvis used it to make over $1,600 on an affiliate program he was promoting.

Understand that Bum Marketing can make you more money from your articles, and it's easy. Don't just use your articles to market your business, turn them into little sales machines that earn you money for years to come. The secret to making a living online and really enjoying your life, as well as find financial freedom is to do the work one time and earn from it over and over. With Bum Marketing and article writing, you can do just that.

Bonus Assignment

1. If you decide to use Bum Marketing as a way to increase your income from article writing, then your first step should be to sign up for the $100 a Day course. It's free, and you can unsubscribe any time. You'll find it here:

http://www.101articles.com

2. If you need a website that will make you money and help you get high rankings in the search engines, sign up for Squidoo and start creating lenses. Once you set them up, you only have to update them about once a month to raise your rankings. Sign up for Squidoo here:

http://www.jingerjarrett.com/recommends/squidoolens.html

3. Don't just write articles; write product reviews. Product reviews are popular online, and you can use them to get more

traffic to your affiliate programs, make more sales, and earn more money.

Notes

Bonus Tip
Getting Your
Articles Listed on
Google News and
Yahoo News

Getting listed on Yahoo News and Google News is a whole lot easier than you think. All it takes is a little research on your part. (This tip also works with MSN News, but it's a lot harder because MSN doesn't index as many sites as Google and Yahoo do).

The first thing you want to do is research. Start with the news sites:

Google News - http://news.google.com/

Yahoo News - http://news.yahoo.com/

First, let's start with Google News.

The first search you want to do is for your topic.

For example, if you're looking for sites that accept health articles, news, or press releases, then search for "health". Browse the listings looking for sites that will accept your content.

Good examples will be article directories and press release sites. You will also want to look for newspapers in your area where you can submit.

One site that accepts articles on just about any topic is Live Articles: **http://www.livearticles.org**. Another advantage to this site is that it offers revenue sharing with Google Adsense, so if you have a Google Adsense account, make sure you add your Adsense ID.

Let me caution you here: when you submit, submit a good article. Use the tips included in this report. You are submitting to get as much free publicity as you can. Don't submit PLR or junk articles full of affiliate links. Most sites won't accept articles that have anchor text for the hyperlink. You have to make the hyperlink the anchor text to get it accepted unless the site doesn't accept links in the body. Then you just have to leave them out.

You can also search for article directories, as well as press releases. This will help you find a lot of sites you can submit to.

Yahoo News not only carries news, but it also carries blogs and forums.

You should search Yahoo News the same way you searched Google News: by keyword. With both sites, if you use a keyword phrase instead of just a keyword, you need to put the phrase in quotes so that you get more relevant results.

One site that is featured at Yahoo News is Ezine Articles, **http://www.ezinearticles.com**. You can submit articles here.

Now, make a list of the sites you have found that accept articles and are listed in Google and Yahoo News. Periodically submit your articles to these sites for additional publicity.

Conclusion

When writing articles, don't forget to include search engine optimization as part of your strategy. This is very important.

For more help on writing articles, as well as free internet marketing techniques, you can read my blog, Internet Marketing for Free, http://www.askjinger.com. You'll find plenty of free ebooks, ecourses, software, tutorials, and other resources to help you.

You can view my latest ebooks, booklets, and my books and CDs on how to market on the internet for free at my main site: .http://www.jingerjarrett.com

If you have questions, you can contact me through support here: http://www.jingerjarrett.com/support/

If you'd like even more free resources to teach you about article writing, as well as starting a business or marketing on the internet, then visit my other sites. You'll find free ebooks and software you can download directly from the site, or you can sign up for my courses.

101 Articles - http://www.101articles.com/ - $100 a Day Ecourse.

Affiliate Marketing – http://www.jingerjarrett.ws – Get your free ebook, Affiliate Money Machine, and learn how to market affiliate programs without a list or website. You'll also learn how to start generating income in seven days or less.

Killer Marketing Arsenal -
http://www.killermarketingarsenal.com/ - Internet Marketing.

Marketing for Writers -
http://www.marketingforwriters.com/ - Marketing and writing related articles and resources.

Small Business How To -
http://www.smallbusinesshowto.com/ - Business, marketing, copywriting, and website building and hosting articles and resources.

Thank you for taking the time to read this course. I wish you the best of luck in writing your articles, and I hope you make a lot of money.

Updates

Occasionally I find additional resources you may find helpful that I haven't added to the ebook. These resources include article writing software, as well as online tools you can use to help you with writing articles. You can find those resources here:

http://www.jingerjarrett.com/lists/articlewritingcourse.html

.

www.ingramcontent.com/pod-product-compliance
Lightning Source LLC
Chambersburg PA
CBHW051237170526
45165CB00004B/1460